MW00804350

A Cuddly Collection of
Fur and Friendship

Cate Holly

RUNNING PRESS
PHILADELPHIA · LONDON

© 2014 by Running Press
Published by Running Press,
A Member of the Perseus Books Group

All rights reserved under the Pan-American and International Copyright Conventions
Printed in China

This book may not be reproduced in whole or in part, in any form or by any means, electronic or mechanical, including photocopying, recording, or by any information storage and retrieval system now known or hereafter invented, without written permission from the publisher.

Books published by Running Press are available at special discounts for bulk purchases in the United States by corporations, institutions, and other organizations. For more information, please contact the Special Markets Department at the Perseus Books Group, 2300 Chestnut Street, Suite 200, Philadelphia, PA 19103, or call (800) 810-4145, ext. 5000, or e-mail special.markets@perseusbooks.com.

ISBN 978-0-7624-5196-8
Library of Congress Control Number: 2013945754

E-book ISBN 978-0-7624-5197-5

9 8 7 6 5 4 3 2 1
Digit on the right indicates the number of this printing

Cover and interior design by Jason Kayser
Edited by Jordana Tusman
Typography: Avenir and Rockwell

Running Press Book Publishers
2300 Chestnut Street
Philadelphia, PA 19103-4371

Visit us on the web!
www.runningpress.com

For SJ, the sweetest kitten of them all.

Introduction

WHAT could possibly be cuter than a super-fluffy kitten with big, green, cuddle-me eyes? Well, how about a little teeny bunny, impossibly furry, with a sweet little crinkly nose? Nothing could be cuter than that, right? Okay, how about a little kitten *and* a tiny bunny all snuggled up together in a basket—and the little bunny has one ear covering the kitten's left eye and the kitten has one paw draped over the fluffy bunny's little bunny bottom. Could there ever be anything even remotely as cute as that?

The truth is, bunnies and kitties have battled for adorableness supremacy through the ages. Ancient Roman texts refer to gladiator-style contests between these combatants of cute. Fluffed up to twice its normal size, a kitten would pounce on a yarn ball or fall over backward while trying to reach for a feather dangling from a thread. His floppy-eared adversary would counter by twitching her nose or, uh, just adorably hopping around. Isn't being cute talent enough?

Some books are depositories of timeless wisdom. Some concern themselves with the loftiest aspects of the human condition. Clearly, this is not one of those books. If you're seeking enlightenment or yearning for answers to life's big questions, quietly close the cover and run away. But if you're looking for the kind of unrelenting and shameless sweetness that takes you to the very brink of sucrose poisoning, the kind of cuteness that threatens to fix your mouth in a permanent state of smiling, well friend, this is the book for you.

Admittedly, books including adorable pictures of kittens have been published before. Bunnies, too, have graced the pages of small but important literary works throughout history. But, here, within these pages, and quite possibly for the first time ever, are presented the two standard bearers of cuddly, the two paragons of lovability: kitties *and* bunnies—together at last.

Fasten your seatbelt, dear reader, it's about to get seriously cute up in here.

When we put our
cute little heads
together, we can think
up all kinds of
ways to get
into trouble. . . .

Keep your friends close and
your best friends closer.

When prepping
for a picnic,
don't forget to pack
plenty of cute!

No, we're not twins . . . but we get that a lot.

With a friend,
you always
have a
place to flop.

Friends like you don't just
flutter by every day.

Keep calm and
be fluffy.

When rough winds
blow, you've always
been my rock.
My big, furry rock.

Two's company . . . three's even better company!

Good friends
are always
home when you
need them.

If black cats are bad luck and rabbits' feet are good luck, you and I had better stick together.

Cute only gets you so far . . . but maybe that's far enough!

Whenever you're around, things start looking up.

Let's hear
it for blended
families!

You're more than a friend…
…you're also a pillow.

Seriously, we're so cute we should refuse to go out in public unless we're getting paid.

We'll be friends
forever . . . as
long as you remember
who's boss.

Hares looking at you, kid.

There's a
fine line between
cute and
claustrophobic.

When you need to
hide from the world, I'll always
give you cover.

I can't help it, I find
you endlessly fascinating.

Life's a movie.
Snuggle
through the
scary parts.

It's what's
between
the ears that
counts.

Frolic, romp, snack,
repeat!

I'm always
here if you need
a comforting
paw.

And I thought *I* was fluffy. . . .

Always
realize when
you're looking
at a phony.

Sometimes you
just have to close your
eyes and leap.

Anyone up for
Duck, Duck, Goose?

When in doubt,
nap about it.

I, Fluffykins, solemnly swear to uphold the vows of the Ancient Order of the Ridiculously Cute.

What would you call it if
three bunnies hopped backward?
A receding hare line.

We're tired of being called cute—
we're frickin' adorable!

If snuggling is wrong, I don't want to be right.

So nice to
know you're always
watching out
for me.

Isn't morning breath
the worst?

Ain't nobody
here but us bunnies.

Somebody
get this
kid a
teddy bear.

What can we say?
We're *gourd*geous.

They say, face your fears,
but what if your fears are just
really freaky strange?

It's a big world out there.
Glad I have you to
explore it with.

Friends don't push.
They gently redirect.

Rabbit? No, we haven't
seen any rabbit. Not around here.
Nope.

Certain types just seem to attract a lot of attention.

I know I can be a little cheeky sometimes, but I just can't help myself.

Do I love you?
Let me sleep on it.

Uh-uh.
I don't smell a thing.

Nothing comes between me
and my honey bunny.

You must have seriously strong genes.

A true friend
doesn't mind if
you bend her ear once
in a while.

Gotta admit, we'd make a pretty striking couple.

If cute were cash, we'd
be stinkin' rich. (But we'll hafta
settle for stinkin' cute.)

You think it's easy being this adorable?

Everyone deserves a little pampering now and then.

Simon says
raise your
left ear if you like
cabbage.

You just can't hide cuteness like yours.

Things always seem to get more interesting when you walk into a room.

When it comes to you, others pale in comparison.

I swear I could just look at you for days.

Size doesn't matter—
it's cuteness that counts.

Sometimes nothing
feels quite right
in my life . . .
except the *you* part
of my life.

Life's a dance.
The trick
is finding the right
partner.

Who says you can't be cute and dignified at the same time?

Friends
can never
be too close.

Raise your paw if you believe
in the Easter Bunny.

You're kinda funny-looking, but you sure are cute.

If I had nine lives, I'd want to spend them all with you.

Shredded sofa? Chewed up veggie garden? We have no idea what you're talking about.

If it's true that we are judged by the company we keep, I'm definitely keeping company with you.

When our gang gets together, it's a wall of cute.

Ever try to do "the wave" with your ears? Not easy.

The first time
I saw you
I knew you were
something
special.

It's a jungle out there . . . let's stay in here.

Hey, are you doing something different with your hare?

Any mice?

No. Any carrots?

No.

Keep looking.

Head to
head, heart
to heart, friends
forever.

You're not just cute,
you're talented too!

Not quite fifty shades of grey, but between us we come close.

Do you believe in
soul mates?

Stick with me, kid,
and I'll make you a star.

You and me . . . the most natural
thing in the world.

Feeling frazzled? Stressed out?
Call The Cute Squad!

Nothing like
having a good pal
on your side.

Every group has its joker.

Guess who's been watching too much wrestling?

Even with a phony background, being adorable comes naturally.

First one to blink is out. Go!

You're so cute sometimes
I swear I could just eat you up.

It's true:
You are kind of a
big deal.

So glad we found each other.

Is this
too close?
Tell me if I'm
getting
too close.

Don't get me wrong. I love fluffy. I'm pretty fluffy myself—but you're kind of off the charts.

Every cool cat needs a solid wingman.

If life's a race, I want to run it with you.

This is just like the savannah and
I am the mighty lioness.
I'm not sure what you are.

I can't sleep.
Would you mind shifting a
little to the left?

Ninety-five percent
of the time, there's
nothing that a well-directed
snuggle can't fix.

I'd do anything for you . . .
but I won't become a vegetarian.

If adorable were a crime, we'd be doing twenty years to life.

Don't care what people say,
we fit together perfectly.

If there's a downside to being adorable it is that one must occasionally sacrifice a little dignity.

Face life without you? Uh-uh, no way. Not gonna happen. Ever.

Friendship is the
ultimate adventure.

I don't care where we're going in a hand basket . . . as long as we're going together.

Don't forget to
be fluffy.

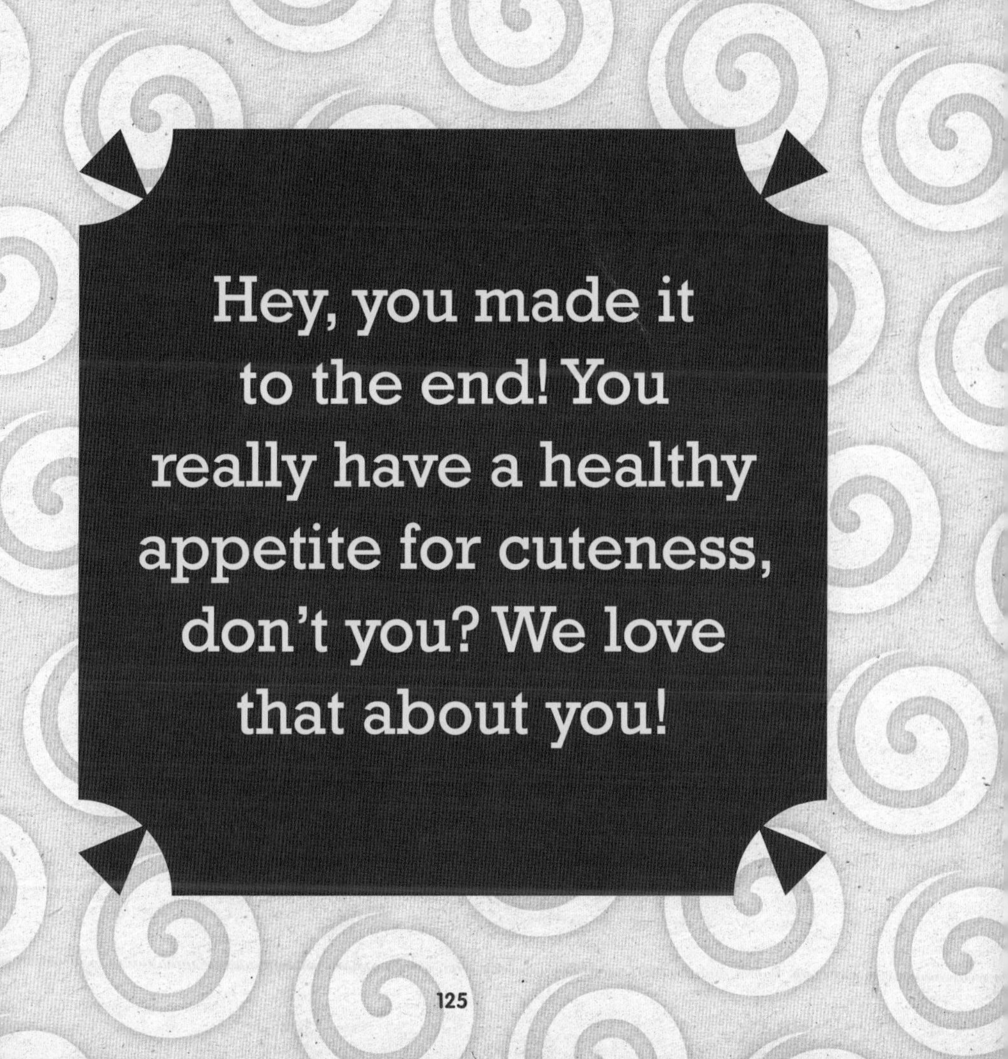

Hey, you made it to the end! You really have a healthy appetite for cuteness, don't you? We love that about you!

THE END

Photo Credits

NaturePL/SuperStock: Front cover, 6–7, 11, 19, 21 (top & bottom), 51, 54–56, 58–60, 62–66, 68, 70–73, 75, 77–78, 80, 82–84, 108, 127

Fotosearch/SuperStock: Back cover (left & center), 8, 50, 52, 61

©iStock.com/101cats: Back cover (right), 23

imagebroker.net/SuperStock: 9

Vaclav Volrab/Shutterstock: 12–13

Linn Currie/Shutterstock: 14, 29, 76

kuban girl/Shutterstock.com: 15, 22, 24, 46

Image Source/SuperStock: 16, 34, 38–39 (top & bottom), 41, 43, 45, 47

Biosphoto/SuperStock: 17, 36

Eric Isselee/Shutterstock.com: 18

Chirtsova Natalia/Shutterstock.com: 20, 53, 57

Dmitry Kalinovsky: 25

Pressmaster/Shutterstock.com: 26

Ermolaev Alexander/Shutterstock.com: 28, 32

Juniors/SuperStock: 30, 37, 40, 42, 86, 88–90, 92–100 (top), 101, 120–122

Animals Animals/SuperStock: 33

NHPA/SuperStock: 35

Biosphoto/SuperStock: 36

Frank Lukasseck/Mauritius/SuperStock: 44, 48

age fotostock/SuperStock: 49

©iStock.com/kuban_girl: 69, 104–105, 111

©Arco Images GmbH/Alamy: 85

©iStock.com/Dixi: 100 (bottom), 112

©iStock.com/Okea: 102

©iStock.com/stanley45: 103

©iStock.com/ptaha_c: 106

©iStock.com/Lilun–Li: 107

©iStock.com/sazonov: 109

©iStock.com/drop-off-dean: 110

©Prisma Bildagentur AG/Alamy: 113

©Juniors Bildarchiv GmbH/Alamy: 114

©Trinity Mirror/Mirrorpix/Alamy: 116

©iStock.com/svetikd: 117

©Tierfotoagentur/Alamy: 118

©iStock.com/fotojagodka: 124